AMERICA
FEBRUARY

AMERICA

W͟M.
KIST-
-LER

Council Oak Books, Tulsa

FEBRUARY

COUNCIL OAK BOOKS

1428 South St. Louis

Tulsa, Oklahoma 74120

1-800-247-8850

In Oklahoma 918 / 587-6454

FAX 918 / 583-4995

ISBN 0-933031-40-8

Library of Congress Catalog Number 91-070168

Design by Carol Haralson

FOR BILL, FOR BRIAN, FOR JIM, FOR LOUISE

with special gratitude to
Alexandra O'Karma
Paulette Millichap
Carol Haralson
Helen Handley
Hayden Carruth
Andra Samelson
Elizabeth Kray Ussachevsky
Elizabeth Hardwick
Daniel Halpern
Amy Bartlett
Cristy West
Elizabeth Dixon
Ann Azulay
Antaeus Magazine, publisher of
   "Mountain Speech Sung as Indian"
Poetry Flash, publisher of
   "Shostakovich, 2nd Movement,
   Quartet No. 7"
Poetry U.S.A., publisher of
   "In the Place of Country"

CONTENTS

THE RIGHT AND LEFT OF MODERN TIMES

MID-WINTER, MANHATTAN

THE PLACE OF COUNTRY

the struggle between the puritan
technological society
and the rapture of the universe
GALWAY KINNELL

The full end of art is not to imitate
a fixed material condition
but to represent a living motion
GEORGE INNES

THE RIGHT AND LEFT OF MODERN TIMES

EXPATRIOT: Bakersfield - Nicaragua: 1963

For what may now have been centuries
I have been getting up from coming
somewhere to plant. For what may now
have been millennia I have been lying down
from going somewhere to pick. And nothing
of rest, no peace, only this bending,
this cutting, and sometimes a single vision,
Luis, how he stood and went down standing.

Myself, working in sight of these Sierras
on this soil so different from our own,
I never can forget any of that past.
In the mornings before the sun, in day,
in even the evenings late, each lost
face returns, and on Sundays I search
in the neon of these towns for some one
of them. Drink. Seek memory. Height

of our hill and the fields like hands upon
the stairs of the sun. The corn in rows,
the mangoes, the coconuts, the almond
and hazelnuts, standing side by side
or wound in as forest and growing wild.
Nothing there but what the earth provides,
nothing of these chemicals, strawberries
at Christmas, asparagus in March,

which I am tending for people distant.
Only our own, grown as Luis said,
by those who eat. Some say he lives,
others that it is his brother. Myself,
I know he knew our life, the slow,
persistent step of our people. Myself,
riding out early in the board of trucks,
coming back late to the board of shacks,

standing shoeless in the dust, standing
rooted in mud, I think only to return.
And if they are waiting, the black hats,
the Civil Guard, up quickly out of
the squad-voice of their barracks, if I
go down, then there I go down. Yet
we know those streets, they will need
many. Jose, Armando, our own will rise,

take what they have hidden and take
from the fallen, we will take them.
Or, lost in the smoke of explosion,
no one will come. They will look out
through their thinnest cracks, turn,
speak nothing. No one will come,
we will pass there unmet and home
on the hard and worn rock of our stone.

MOUNTAIN SPEECH SUNG AS INDIAN

I am the one, I am the only one
who ever left and went below and worked
and learned what they know and returned.
Now I understand how electric light shines
like fire but does not die and how metal
frames which have no legs run forward

and back. Now I am back, the one man
going up the mountains in the morning
with the women and the llamas
and waiting and coming down as the sun
sinks and leaves us alone with the moon
and the slow-changing face of the stars.

These are our mountains. Pizarro
has come on his burro with the priests,
and Ernesto Guevara with his beard
and piercing eyes reaching for death.
Each had his beliefs and the force
of his demands, neither knew our lives.

We are woven into these clouds, just
as the daisies whose short-stemmed faces
grow as large as clay cups, each finger-
end balancing and casting its shadow
on the frost earth beside the mossy rocks
where lichen nest and drop their spore

into the open fissures and seams.
My first sister and our second sister
weave as they walk and graze the llamas
along the upper mountain, their hunger
leading them slowly, continuously, through
the sparse grass, our bright ribbons hanging

motionless in the mane of their necks.
My first sister carries the loom
on her back, its braces and staves
wrapped with red bands and curving
over her shoulders and around her waist.
Our second sister walks behind, shifting

the wool, working the shuttle, adding
strand by strand to the rust-brown blanket.
Step beside step, only in harmony,
they go on in the high air, under
the sun-mottled sky, surrounded by stones
and the pure, thin, tooth-like click

of wood striking cleanly on wood.
Looking off and far down from the edge
of this terrace I can see the triangular
inclined stone of our roofs with their
arching ovens of pebbles and dung pellets.
Smoke is not rising and no one inside

is sleeping on the earth pallets
we have built above the earthen floor
where our guinea pigs shift and turn
like tassels of corn loose on the wind.
We eat their grey meat roasted
over fires of burning llama dung.

We eat our llamas also but only
when they are old. We have lived too close,
each looking into the other's eyes
as we sheared their wool and drank
their milk. We are drunk and cannot sing
when, at last, we have to kill them.

Season into the same season we eat
the cabbages and corn and turnip-like
quetzoal and orange sweet potatoes which
we plant at the bottom of the eastern
slopes, down at the edge of the jungle
where the broad rivers gather and begin.

We stay, we camp there and tend them
until harvest and we return to the women
and the walk of the mountains. And at day's
end, just before the same hour of always
the same equatorial sunset, we cross to bathe
where the cold and the hot streams meet.

Warm, smelling of the mountain, we rise
out of the rising steam. And now it is
the hour of fire and the night of song
and Fierce Owl and Word of the Wind
let free from the burnished stems
of their pipes their jagged harmonies

so much like the up and down lines
of our mountains. They play their rhythms
of breath into each of our lives, we flow
into the voice of one another. There is
no theft, we sing, and there is no hoarding
of Gold, there is no valuing and there is

no violence, in the home, in the continuing
home of these mountains. You will not
take us back with you as photographs
and we will not accept instruction,
whether Spanish or Cuban, whether Pizarro
speaking from pulpit or Guevara

slowly dying in the lung as martyr.
We have gone down and we have seen
the hunger and the great wealth lust.
We have squatted down in Cuzco
under our own ages of fitted stone
and we have seen the fastened faces

dark as forest rain where they sit
and count paper and move numbers.
We and the llama and the dung
we and the cabbages and the streams
we and the wool and the looms
now and now and now are one.
And nothing will move us.
And no one will ever move us.

GANDHI IN SOUTH AFRICA

Without praise or blame, without
anger or defeat, after the officer
had delivered a blow to the side
of his bare shaved head, he folded
the disordered clothes, placed
them in the cardboard suitcase.

One side locked fully. He wrapped
his belt tight around the other
as blood spread down over the bone
line of his cheek. He had hoped
to call forth non-violent commitment.
He had not. His arm lifted

the bound suitcase as his friends
and fellow citizens stood to the side.
The shape of the truth of one race
abusing another, opened and filled
their minds, went all the way through
into the center of their imagining.

Not one of them could step away
from that seamless wall of silence.
He walked on across the road as fear
and inchoate anger dripped hatred
into their hearts, and the clubs
of the soldiers were slowly lowered.

We know now that almost all of them
turned and later joined him. Some
small measure of freedom shimmered
before them, gradually was taken,
changed by degrees the reach
of their day to day perceptions.

SHOSTAKOVICH, 2ND MOVEMENT, QUARTET NO. 7

Note by note, chord by slower by darker by
lower chord, he took himself down into each
whispered strand of despair, down entirely into
the sightless, tomb-like cavern of organized,
bureaucratic murder. No one else would ever

descend far enough to convey that pulsing
furnace fire of the state, the mind of vengeful,
lost Stalin lying alone in the darkness
of his room. He himself, Dimitri Shostakovich,
died from progressive heart failure

and the advancing hunger of multiple tumors.
Between blocked arteries and the suffocation
of vital organs, his own irreconcilable sadness
at the fate of those around him, gave up
its place, imagined itself asleep on the floor

in the depths of Siberian winter, dreamt
of eternal spring, joined his cousin Kostya
in the shackled silent standing of forced
labor. Each of them was frozen there,
was left faceless, inert, beyond any caring

or inspiration, lumped together as one
with Mandelstam the poet whose Yiddish-
Russian words were as intense as his lined face,
the electrical engineer who had lived upstairs,
the Menshevik democrats of 1905 who still
in the cells of their hearts were socialists.

THE JAIL AT THE END OF MEMORY

I am alone on the floor, no bed only concrete.
I have not eaten for what seems like months
but once were days, time without the barest
syllable of shape as I drink their soot-filled
water and eat the rounded corners of my own

silence. It is clear now that they are going
to kill me, but by degrees, more slowly
than this beetle which I hold like an egg
in the motionless, air-like calm of my hand.

I am no longer present, only these teeth
that grind this stiff skeleton, this tongue
which takes down his dark juices, my lost
stomach which wakes and howls all night
at such an incomprehensible blending of fates.

Isn't there somewhere a second, a third, any
other room into which I can one day awake?

A CORNER OF THE NEW WORLD

You are young, you're sitting in a chair,
your crime was that you had meetings
with people who believed in free elections.
You are young, you're tied to a chair,
they are going to put wires under your nails,
one by one. What was your crime? You believed
in at least some land to those who farm.

And the implementer of unprintable tortures,
what life does he say that he believes in?
His pay, his uniform which marks him
as a Captain, the smooth legs of both
of his mistresses. And the General?

Land for each of his children, his collection
of the totemic carvings of native Indians
who are in revolt down on the coast, his
pictures of women bent over without clothes
or tied in chairs with their legs spread.

You are young, you're tied to a chair,
your head is covered with a metal bucket,
they are hitting it with large sticks.
What did you believe in? Not simply
the Brotherhood of man, but the dignity
of women, men, the whole living, unfinished
family of us. And the President, asleep

in his protected morning, what does he say
he believes in? Economic aid in the form
of tanks, mortars. Position papers which state
each person's right to basic human rights.
You are young, you're sitting in a chair, you
also believed in human rights, they now want
the names of each of your friends. And myself,

poet, collector of the facts which reflect
the mind of the present? I was once a diplomat.
I wrote under the Spanicized name of a Dutch
Caravagiste painter, Gerard de la Noce.
Like him I was a realist who began to see
only in the darkness. Now I am old.

I still believe in the one spot of earth
under the one tree in our small garden.
I drink once a month with the Prime Minister.
We talk international finance. We drink
and recite nineteenth-century love poems
and sing the perfectly remembered songs of youth.

I am old, I am tied to this many-roomed house.
I think of my wife, silent in her black hair,
as full as the earth in the ochre, the umber,
the burnt sienna which met in her eyes.
I am old, I am haunted by the voices
of neighbor children chasing and running
like the several paths of a mountain stream.

I am old. Every day on my own body
I find and bring into honor some small wound
or swollen tear in order to feel again,
feel from within a hidden, a not lost,
not forgotten pain as of suffering. Truly
I am old, I am tied to these fading curtains

rustling by the window. I have stopped
eating the flesh of birds and cattle,
I take as little of everything else
as possible. I kill only rats, cockroaches,
they are no longer innocent but think
in aggressive patterns like us. I am old,

 I am tied to this many-roomed house. You
are young, you're tied to a chair. We each
believed in at least some land to those
who farm. I swear that I will try in words,
in thought, without anger, to change them.
I swear I will go on speaking the names
of each part of this broad humanity
which we both once believed we belonged to.

THE RIGHT AND LEFT OF MODERN TIMES

My brother spoke and said it was not his,
why did we worry it would never be our own,
as we watched the grey pike fish gasp and sink
beyond the chain-like fence and telephone wires
where the congealing rain opened softly,
peppered down, joining the thickened waters.

It rained and it flecked with circle patterns
the tinted windows of the black limousine as the
wine glasses sighed with the splash of champagne.
They were drinking at dusk as the lake lay flat
before them and the driver snuffed his cigarette,

turned to watch the front seat television,
bending forward, tuning the Rock Concert,
while they talked international video finance.

There is not any poverty in the free economy,
every man a king unless the market passed him over
or he was born a fish and poisoned under
the shadow of coal ash being converted to fuel
for glass fabrication in the cathode ray tube plant.

They go on smoking and drinking and adding plans
as long as the money is moving and spreading demand
and fear is felt in the common heart of turning
off the light alone in the dark and falling
to sleep without the well-known voices of songs
and the insistent constancy of advertising.

And just at that same moment, in the workers'
welfare state, the plant manager is failing his quota
as the foreman sits down to a cigarette, switches
the Japanese Sony to the afternoon talk show.
It isn't, certainly, the same as last year

now that the wheat crop fell under forecast
and foreign earnings dropped and the French champagne
had to be left off the import list, leaving
just this Slivovitz and these memories of the Fifties
with their interminable importunings across
every channel of this workers' watcherless television.

AMERICAN ZEC

I, who enlarged the universe 100,000 times,
am shrunk to the size of my own body.
GALILEO GALILEI

A piece of warm, multi-grain bread
and when I eat I hold no thought
but of this life enclosed in death.
A polished car, and when I drive
upon the banked highway with still

a clear passage of signal lights,
I find no thought but of the force
of death presenting itself as weapon
and taking its form as weapon, as when
a shell explodes, scatters, lungs, heart,

every blood-filled organ of a life,
as far as its broken metal parts.
At work, seated in buffed leather
with a thick alphabet of telephones,
teleterminals, I can frame no print

but of the gaunt, the worm-eaten,
the tunnelled collapse, where only
stubborn, virulent viruses remain,
devour me whole from the inside
without any thought of laughter.

Every advance must consume itself,
myself, functionary that I now am
within this lighted case of my life,
I think I will try sky diving, sign
tomorrow with the department of fire.

POTATOES WAKING

At the end of the student dance they drew
open the brown bag, let potatoes bounce
and scatter along the length of the stage.
Then they moved among them, picking them up,

throwing them two, three, four at once, back
into the burlap. They moved quickly while
the audience smoked, discussed the performance.
Potatoes landed in darkness, lay crooked

against each other. New hands took the bag,
flung it out from the stage. No one caught it
as it fell across the canvas of the backdrop.
The dancers at last came forward, began again.

Each of us at the end departed, rode home
in cars. As if they had returned to a life
set in a separate place, the bruised eyes
of potatoes turned inward, looked back into

the dance of humans, saw that they had been
props left behind in burlap, brought there
from earth, from the dark place where the soft
heads of worms and the forefeet of moles

had pushed close, had waited for some small
movement in the soil, then had receded
like a sudden departure of rain or spring.
This place also was dark but with a hardness

they had not known. Slowly they found them-
selves drawn toward the tangles of dust lying
in every corner, found themselves wanting

to be covered, felt the molecular life
within them stir, reach wordlessly about,
seek the close and ordinary warmth of earth.

THIS PRESENT

The bang-banging of trains in the tunnel.
Nowhere to sit, we are standing. Others,
thin, drenched in sweat, lean against us.
No one talks. I lift the pins from her hair,
let the reddish-black strands fall down full

onto her shoulders. Back we return in mind,
further back than this train, than this work
we maintain as we cross, recross, in the half-
steps of routine through buildings where each
window completes an even, air-conditioned room.

There never were doors open to memory or longing
within those walls, and electric bulbs fade
beside the subtle lights of sense which spread
from each end of her fingers as she lifts
her long hair pins from the palm of my hand

and we step out into the traffic of the streets,
into this lobby with one rubber plant, onto
this corridor painted one dim color. This time
enter this room without light, only reflections
rising through blinds. Stand without speech.

Sit in the overstuffed chair. Watch shadows
mirror the street. Somewhere my tie is loose,
now her shoes. Somewhere my chest can breath,
now her feet. Each limb is separate, has
become a person, all of their eyes are alive.

AMERICA FEBRUARY

February again, presenting the winter
of my forty-first year, with its trees
that are dim-standing and the grey-white
haze of snow lying opaque where he is.

No epitaph on the cut stone: William Kistler
1910 - 1960. No home where it was
auctioned column by cornice down to its base,
and no business where it was stripped

and sold for salvage to strangers.
No wife where she died in a fire of cancer,
and his sons and his daughter dark in debt
and gone out abroad where they dispersed.

This is America February. 14 degrees
fahrenheit, 29.4 pounds barometric pressure,
wind, north/northeast, 13 miles per hour.
Cold, clearing and we are measuring.

And a thousand times a thousand we are
moving in the bristle edge of winter
and the open-in warmth of summer where
the clothes are taken off and for an hour

we feel free, though still in motion.
And you must move to keep buying
and you must sell to keep moving,
and the cars are driving into the shopping

center to buy and the shopping center
is unrolling its asphalt tundra alongside
the rising highway and there is no hunger
of stomach we have not shaped and cannot own.

And as we turn through the photographs of youth
only the full simplicity of his face
and the pressed cloth of his clothes
hold against the corrosion of age.

The actual passing moments of his living
have dissolved in the throat of time
and we are left with June 16, 1912, where
silver tinted and yellowing in daguerreotype,

he is two years past the day of his birth.
The first cubist collages are being born
at that same moment in the building called
The Floating Laundry. Diaghilev,

Stravinsky and Fokine are preparing the four
acts of Petrouchka, the puppet victim,
the sufferer at the power of the more powerful,
the loser in the tenderness of his own soul.

And Bill Kistler standing knock-kneed,
uncertain and shoeless in short pants,
is moving his hand through space to a chair,
his eyes looking out to question how.

April 1917 and he is tall in trousers,
posing almost military at attention
with the wheeled frame of his bicycle.

Thousands are plunging through the open
door of death in fear and in shock,
their souls and furthest memory lost
to the life of their bodies and falling

back across time suddenly and without harmony
as automatic weapons fire World War One lead
at uncontrollable rates. Picasso, Cocteau,
Satie and Massine are creating the forms

for the movement of the new century
in the towers and walking typewriters
of the jazz, cubist dance-ballet, Parade.
They are gone now, the framers of the pure line

and moving geometry of the twentieth century.
He is gone too. And though they spoke for him
in a way he did not understand and though
he lived in a commerce they could not accept,

they were of the same urban, individual,
democratic freedom. Grain to our grain, but
darker more determined in their discovering
of the hidden shapes of the spirit. Each thing

manufactured or natural, as they knew then,
is living. But we have grown younger,
are more covered and more taken in these
streaming ready-mades of city, myriad,

growing, and drawing the force of our lives
into their ceaseless life of payment. I hear
Fokine shaping movement. I see Petrouchka
turn in the dance. Bill Kistler is watching.

Come down into us you who went before. Bless,
sing to us. Tell us of the free, independent,
inner flowing strength we feel and always
and again are about to join, letting the mind

open, go by degrees into the skull-dark,
cell-clear length of its field. Lie silent
in a field of remembering. Lie alone in a light
unhindered. Ripen past need, grow beyond loss,

live close in and far off, on its own
and for itself, in each curve of knowledge,
each hinge and crossing of interior
where corridors of seeking rest and meet.

There we might lean back, remain at peace,
through the day of work, the shade of evening,
as the streets, the lights and the selling

spread their magnetic net of signs
and we open the car door, turn the brake,
ride forth sack in hand to buy.

MID-WINTER,
MANHATTAN

LINES WRITTEN FROM A RESTAURANT
ON THE CORNER

I was late getting out of court,
we did not meet in the restaurant.
And though we had hardly known each other,
no more than one very direct conversation

where the words were like stones we might use
to build a room, a temporary shelter,
which each of us could enter and which
we were relieved not to finish, with, as it were,

nothing but words between us, still I remembered
I had wanted to follow the rope of her voice
through the doors and into the suggested corridors
of her mind, feel her eyes examine my face,

construct perhaps a house which this time
would speak with the life of windows.
I dialed her number. I heard her voice.
It breathed the simplicity - less is inevitably

more - which I believed I had understood.
She would come over. No complaints. No shards
of unspoken unhappiness at having had to wait.
What, I wondered, would she be wearing?

It was just the restaurant on the corner.
Would she likely have earrings hidden
in the curling, impossible to find an order,
tumult of her hair, or, would there be the bright,

flowering border of a scarf coming down
to encircle her neck, disappear into her coat?
I shifted my tie. I took out my comb.
I drowned it in the electric sea of my own hair.

NEAR THE BEGINNING

Memories and the clotted patterns of words
from other, earlier love affairs are scattered
like pollen grains down the forest paths
of our senses. We are each beginning

to feel the life's story of the other
as this room stretches out until it is filled
with carefully mannered men and women.

We continue talking as we dance, and it is
civilized like that until the saxophone
opens a very long note, begins a rhumba
so rhythmic she becomes weightless in my arms.

I let myself go. The white table cloths
disappear, and the faces framed with blue hair,
and the eye glasses fastened to the faces.

This is not a hotel, a ballroom, this is
a falling, or perhaps a stepping to the side,
directly out of sequential time, through
a frameless door we have called a moment.

Somewhere over there, standing as if
in a different light, each of us can see
the primordial lives of first one

and then the other, glowing, transparent,
without fear, without the need of a face.

THE BOWL WHICH THE CANDLE FILLED

The bowl which the candle filled
with yellow shifting light, filled itself
in my hand to the form of her hip.

I began with her foot, the partly hidden
hollow of her ankle, and always at the end
the bowl of her hip lay open in my hand,

that ground where each of our separate
energies met, dissolved. To find myself
linked with her in mind exceeds any

other life except the completion of touch.
We each vote, buy cars, sell whatever
others think they need, until society

has worked its daily, practiced speeches
deeply into us. And just at that moment
when I can no longer believe in the order

shaped by such a life, my hand might
slide across the round back of a chair,
the long curve of her hip returns,

suddenly I am beyond the everyday claims,
our hidden life rises, covers all routine.
And if she ever is gone from me

I will be as alone as Narcissus,
with only my energy as my mirror
and feeling that I have never

but this once, one, unceasing taking
felt at home in the single lake
and river joining of her body, free

as every effort is extinguished and each
moment of continuing lifts itself out
toward its own unknowable future.

WORDS WRITTEN BETWEEN ACTS

She certainly was one who believed,
as almost all women instinctively believe,
that we, men, are placed in life as simple
support to their incomparably greater drama.

It is for each of them to see themselves
as the central actors within the month
to month, year to year, cycles of seed-
bringing and birth, almost the same light

in which we see ourselves as warriors,
touts, rulers of all things living, both
the visible, and the tiny, uncharted,
molecular energy of things invisible.

Tears splashed from her eyes, she scolded
through breakfast, told me I was silent,
dead, uninterested. I found myself
a lost force searching a lost spirit,

I only thought I remembered I once knew.
Tormented, forgetful, Siegfried seeking
Odette in a treeless forest of anger
as the music broke off, left him standing

in the wings. And if I should come forward,
stepping calmly in the blue hour of evening,
offer the one breath of my essence
into her bed, why then it might cloud

the white rose of her table, interrupt
the candlelit dinner before even the wine
is poured down into the wine glass,
the knife sounds aloud on the plate,

the peas meet and overflow the spoon.

MID-WINTER, MANHATTAN

The quarter falls from the roll of bills,
I bend forward to pick it up, she starts
to shout. In the moment of collision

the lady in the car in front suffers
whiplash of the neck. Later it continues,
she tells me I'm a lover of other women,

she has other men, we lead double lives,
it's no good going on, it's finally over.
If, for example, she didn't have to work

at a job which leaves her feeling sick,
if I didn't have to play tennis with angry,
aging sportsmen, in order to sell things

I don't believe in, so taxes can be paid
on things we don't truly need. Is this what
Shakyamuni Buddha meant by the shadow

world of ignorance? Is this the Christian
concept of original sin? Perhaps if I had
brown, tranquil eyes, if I did not have

the out-of-date hungers of a Romantic,
or again, if I were at peace, if she
and the world itself were at peace, then

each of us might remember that we have
known the other as we have known ourselves,
which is to say both before and after

the events of birth, beyond speech, as though
in sleep. In other words, if there were
another universe in a similar place,

recalling itself in a very different way,
the coming together of one with another,
those two in understanding with each

of the others. Untroubled. The continual
swinging low of the still unseen, sweet chariot.

STOPPING IN THE COURT ON FOURTH STREET

I saw it from the street. I walked
into the court. It was not different
from many other autumn trees, only
about a third of its leaves remaining.

Each leaf gone through orange into
a blanched-out yellow brown, the color
of parchment, that texture as of ancient
paper, with overtones of secret,

precious knowledge held in each letter.
Was it the subtle grain of leaves which
brought her presence back to me, or was
she continually there, pushing through

and arriving whenever I might pause
from thought? I had felt closer to her
than any other person I had known.
And now as five or six leaves unhook

from different limbs, several of her
gestures come forward into memory,
follow each leaf downward in a silent
curve of movement which I am still

trying to fasten back, all the way
out of this court, each of us still
trying to walk away from the distant,
final holding we had given each other,

to the side of the crowd, in front
of the theatre, under the airless shine
of arc lights. That was in a time
when I believed that as love ends,

it simply ends, goes out of the heart. Now
I am alone and the truth rests upon me
that the more you might love someone
the more you might hurt them, and the more

you hurt them the more you yourself
would hurt, regret beyond any telling
that you had caused them pain, they alone
in the white of their body's wrapping,

they in the freedom of their gentleness
and bearing the slow-running stream
of their black eyes, they in the diamond-
like clarity of their mind and holding

the pain of the hurt you had given them
and which now you would give each arm
to reverse. That was before. And that was
still before. And none of it would return,

except somewhere in the vaporous evenings
of memory, there unhook and with these leaves
take all of one's life out into the long,
downward sloping angles of its fall.

LETTER TO A DEPARTED DAUGHTER

My daughter, the one continuing female eye
within my life, my daughter, now woman,
all that will go on after me and all that
is known to me, is mine by the indecipherable
locking of conception and yet is not owned
as my own, it was a relief as if in birth
when the doctor loosed the cord between us.
I stepped, I can tell you now, down stairs
glittering with freckled shards of ceramic.

Crossed asphalt hot with the bright metal
of expensive cars, thought there how people
in these consultative sessions of therapy,
even as they try to persuade each other
into and out of the forms of their fates,
are never far off from the terms of trade.
The last thing he sought, you may remember,
was my billing address which we knew he had.

Better we should explore, step into the heat
of uncontrolled change, than continue this
turning over of our own entrails in the name
of science, order. At just about the point
where the granular black of the parking lot
met the smooth cement of the sidewalk, I
let you leave completely into the thickened
light of bars, drugs, whatever else.

It is easy now to tell, but in that knot
of emotion holding us as one I had to search
as if within a densely wooded canyon
for the small path which would lead me out of
fear for you, out of the structure of involvement.
Did I no longer feel myself your father?

Did your insistent, unassuageable energy,
your need to cross to the furthest end of each
strand of your sexual life, leave me feeling
that we were separated by line after white,
powdery line of the Coca plant, the leaves
of which the Quetchua slowly chew, do not refine,
do not seek after aimless feelings of power.

My daughter, my friend, as in the pattern
of plants and all animals, you have gone out
from your mother and myself. We are no longer
separate as older, but simply beside you.
And if you were to ask we could not but say
that you are more distinct, more full of the force
of person, than ever we might have hoped.

We see you and step back. We leave our hands,
just now thin and beginning to wrinkle.
You can turn to them in your mind or pretend
you carry them with you as amulets,
as open charms in the forest of the streets.

I walked on, just as you had warned, there were
no buses. After a time the sidewalk turned,
led under an elevated highway. Dust drifted
down in small puffs onto my suit. Rain fell.

I entered a church I had known long before.
The saints, the few free minds of the past,
Catherine with her spiked wheel, Peter
holding his upside-down cross, each was there
with the instrument of torture which had ended
their search, left them free as white bones
in a white sand field. Anger slowly forced
itself forward bearing the weight of the past.

Did you need to destroy so much of yourself
simply in order to leave? I drew a breath.
I tilted my head as if to look more clearly
into what you had felt. Thin bands of light
crossed the apse from the left, divided
the carved lines of the choir stalls into
equal lengths. I accepted loss brushed clean
in those chords of light. I accepted anger,
let the breath go all the way out of my lungs.

I waited. To breathe was to know the one
rhythm of the living. I had only to stand
or sit, walk out or remain, the same strength
would flow through me. I no longer felt
apart from myself. I brought my head back
into balance. I waited. The altar lamp
went on casting its shadow upon the cross.
Each flower beside the altar stood with each.

You would be as you were, haunted I understood,
by the hidden curve of death which whispers
constantly to each of us like a distant,
departed lover. In the coil of that bond
you might hope one moment would turn fully inward,
open itself in a sharp, awakened ecstasy, or
the cloudy light of dream, startle, set you free.

In the transept, in windows stained the subtle,
passive colors of the spirit, Saint Michael
was sending the spark of unencumbered life
to Mary. Mauves, lavenders, dark blues, sky-
light blues, separate in the portrait, blending
rainbow-like in the air as the sun came out,
shone through. I let my spirit go into them.

I would walk on, buy vegetables, an egg
to boil, eat in honor of the act of eating.
I would wish that you were present in peace,
wish for each of us a beginning, the chance
to write down the letters which make words
which act as signs of the loss of the past.
Write in such fidelity to our struggle

that every line upon each page would ignite,
that each word within each line would link,
that each letter within each word and finally
each of the spaces between the letters between
the words, would settle into themselves, radiate,
as if they were the full hope of this day
printed now in order to be felt, felt again.

TWO TRAVELERS IN PASSING

Dark down in my heart on a cold evening
just at dusk, in that half light which falls
into the street and is held as if it were breath,
I drift in and enter the church of San Sylvester.

Fixed in death, in my own fading speech of flesh,
I look in the chapel ceilings for paintings,
for some sign of the spirit in its fire of sight,
find only the inscriptions and marble caskets

of each generation. I turn, then leave looking
back into candles and flickering shadows,
seem to hear the stirring of covered secrets,
the whispered beseechings of the long-departed.

Now I am out of step, stand almost disembodied
among shoppers moving in the market street.
Cross over. View from the other side the Gothic,
gargoyle-thick bell tower, each step a passage

into the depth of generations who sold here
and bought, and by hand laid the order
of their days into the form of these stones.
Now he is speaking behind my back, asking

for an offering as he pushes forward, the wheels
of his wooden cart jumping and starting
in the ridges of cobblestone. He stretches
his hand as far up and as close to my belt

as he can, raises the shrunken stump of his leg
until it touches my knee. We both are distant
from all of the others when I pass my few coins,
the fierce, pulsing, fatigued face of my eyes

full into his, exchange each hunger of person
between us. Now each of us comes forward
into memory, on just such a crowded evening,
in just such a medieval street where

round wheels caught in stone cracks, released
their hardness of sound all the way across
plazas which dissolved into doorways, stairs,
balustrades. Centuries and centuries of our

two extended lives appearing out of greyness.
Meetings, and the forms of our many faces
and the changing shapes of architecture
appearing, as if our roles were the same

and at the same time capable of being
reversed. Bound in many histories, locked
together in continuing steps, born as one,
there and there within the next and the next,
present into this unending present.

WITHIN THE PASSAGEWAY OF THE LOUVRE

Only a few of us walking in mid-afternoon
through the portico leading to the broad
inner court of the Louvre, stopped to listen
to his playing of Bach's Violin Sonata.

The notes held for many moments, seemed
to place themselves in rows so that I might
feel each suspended beside the other.
Slowly they rose, drifted down the length

of the arches. Almost everyone passing
had cameras, filmed him with deep circles
and the mauve-red color of starvation
etched around his eyes. He was playing

for money but the notes flowed up
from his beginnings. I could feel his past,
each of his lost hopes, lift and go out.
A small woman with twisted fingers, bent,

took several coins from his hat. He shuffled
some steps after her, turned, let his anger
pass. More sadly and with more of the pain
of unearthly longing, he began again.

Now Police came, asking for identification
and speaking on radios. He laid his violin
in the orange velvet of its case, gathered
his jacket up, stepped into a grey rain

falling seamlessly out of a grey sky.
Each of us left alone there, was left
with the passing of many feet and many
voices, all of them rising, turning over,

blending indistinguishably in the spaces
where his notes had spread among the columns,
had released themselves one after another
into the boundless curve of the present,

that place where they might invisibly rest,
as if they had been set down in a life
we could no longer think of as past, as lost,
as fallen into a veil of dark nothingness.

YOU COME TO ME TENTATIVELY

You come to me tentatively, as though
your spirit were wrapped in shadows.
You lift yourself gently as if you barely
know which face it is you might remember.

And when such intricate, slow exchanges
have passed without effort between us,
I feel as if I have been washed and laid
out clean in the depths of the sky,

scattered down all its length with lights
which we continue to think of as stars
but which now we know are the most intense
charges of energy. No living thing

stands against us. If a snake appears
we have only to step around it, or,
if the way is narrow, kill it without anger
or be killed. This life, forming up

and changing itself everywhere around me,
I now understand is but a passage from
one state to another. There is no loss,
no final disappearance. Gradually

I have let go of fear, can see how
you come forward without words, can feel
the distance as it falls away between us,
can feel this calling out within me

like the dark voice of sadness stretched
across a winter sky, can sense this breath
drawing down deeper than hunger as it opens,
goes out toward you, offers each aspect

of myself as if it were a drying leaf,
had no life left but the one it must give
to earth, the one which it seemed it had
known it could lose and still not be lost.

LISTENING

You knelt and looked down into me, your eyes
were richer than even the subtle pages
of your skin. I let each part surround me,
the black pupils, the iridescent, flame-like

strands of the irises. Each dream of each
of my senses recognized itself, became
my mind, became frames of light, dissolved.
Did I believe I knew you? I had known

a daily face. I lay back. I felt myself
a white sheet released fully from print.
I looked at you. My arms lay back.
I went on looking. I wanted never to move.

Joining became like knowing your person
without sight, subtle, slow-changing tides
which shifted in whispers. Neither of us
held the other, only a place angling

then running like a river, which we knew
together. There we began, somewhere
between the fluted dialogue of ecstasy
and the continuous, calm, walking in of peace.

AS SOMETHING DIFFERENT

As something different from the most complete
of friends, you enter the daily pattern
which I have carefully put into order.
And now I understand this is more than chance,

this is my life's reaching toward the never-
found, that presence of woman which it feels
as if I have been continuously seeking, though
also it seems as if it surrounds, as if

you are inside each part of me, and outside
around all of me, like the floating life of air.
The search for the not-found, that blend of person
not yet seen but which the cells of my gene print

continue to whisper must exist. Not simply
black hair and pale skin, not any particular
description, but you, a woman of unambiguous
warmth, wrapped in a robe of measureless calm.

Each aspect of yourself a line drawn down
a strand of beach and feeling as though it might
run on forever, so that like a loving, tribal
mother, you might be large enough to accept

these restless still uncertain parts of myself
which I have not yet brought into balance.
Your warmth and the depth of your peace joined
like the stem and bloom of a living flower,

as if you remembered that you were fully
sentient, might stir like the serrated
edges of a leaf when the breath of my life
has brushed by. All of you your own search,

and held in a body which could stand at ease
in any room, stand as if unhindered
by the demands of the day-to-day, stand
like fruit which has been cut, which spills

its essence bit by bit down through the length
of a cloudless afternoon, down onto a sheet
that does not stop drinking, that is the same
as the hidden unguardable heart of myself.

IN THE CHANGE

A room. A bed. A window looking out
on the broad traffic of a river, much of it
coming in, turning around, going back out,
very little remaining in this trans-port

to the north, the east. Parting we lift
through the last diminishing where the movement
between us ends into finish. Blankets
are thrown back, feet find the floor, up

we rise into the forms of shoes, of clothes.
You are a separate life and distinct,
each thing happening here, happening now to me,
is happening differently over there to you.

I choose an orange. I peel it. I eat.
I let the white insides, clean as this light
from the risen moon, rinse my teeth. I rest.
I let the length of your neck suggest my lips.

You sense them and turn. I feel the hidden
veins of your neck meet my lips, those veins,
that pulsing blood of life, which is choosing
the place toward which you will soon depart.

We wake again into this room through which
we both are looking. Each thing before us,
the rug, the pattern etched into the rug,
the chair resting on the curve of the rug,

seems to be coming out and coming toward us
as if they were emblems of the objects
and the distance which will form between us.
We are not one, we will never be, each life

taking different choices, different countries,
and holding back a hand as this moment
loosens, leaves, goes off into the magnetic,
web-like, horn and bell calls of the river.

PARTING AND BEING APART

Parting, it seemed later, was like
each of us leaving the same station
in opposite directions. Slowly
we were farther apart, not so far

after a while that we couldn't stop,
circle 'round a shale-strewn embankment,
begin walking back, each one toward
the other, eventually meet. But if

too much time went slowly and then
quickly by, before we might know it
we would have gone too far, be too
much to ourselves and with the taste

of too many events in between, to then
be able to find our way back. We are
distant now, one from the other, but
still I would walk through the length

of each night, go on walking, simply
for one look at the varied, asymmetrical
angles of your face, a single taste
offering me both salt and incense.

Hunger, and the humors of passion,
and the memory of ecstasy leading me
to a height from which I might understand
these few, infrequent, almost random

meetings, which draw us together, then
after a time, as if we had stood
too near the sun, inexplicably force us
apart. Walking. And I am still walking.

As I am closer, or is it farther,
I ask the dawn to wait, for if this night
does ever end, you may melt, be lost, be
beyond reach, not here, nearly in sight.

FIRST LINES OF ORPHEUS

Now I am withdrawn all the way out of life,
find myself dreaming like a child or someone
very old. Now without fear of being alone

I lie down in a fresh bed, which looks onto
an empty room, where as the sun departs
I will soon step. Stay in that unfettered space,

never look back but wish for you, Persephone,
the arrival of the colors of your full person,
Spring. For myself I choose the varied greys

of this place where each word is a leaf
branching from its source, each sentence
a landscape of first meanings. The whole

an origin from which the subtle linkings
of idea rise, go forth. Here I can continue
beside you, feel you within the two-sided

consciousness of song — myself thinking
of the many edges of your person as I
sing of your youth — see you now in the place

I once knew as my heart. Beyond flesh,
and freed of each of the sacred, chord-like,
soundings of passion, this has become

my deepest strength, reaching out to you
through floors and into the earth, into
what I once thought were the inviolate

boundaries of the dark world, of winter,
of snow bringing its white crystals forward
out of the loom of rain, out of the wordless

faces of death, so that in every one
of the lives I enter in song, I see his face
woven into trees, into cars, into the ashy

smoke of coal where it blends with the morning
mist, even into the bread mix flowing back
before the spoon, as it whirls, turns over,

looks directly at me, as though I also
held the incandescent torch of life.

THE PLACE
OF COUNTRY

LIFE IN THE STUDY

The petals were bent outward
like tears that we might imagine
holding to the edge of heaven.

They fell from the tulip stems
in spare, curvilinear sequences,
one, and one, two. I felt them

upon the floor, breathing less
and then less. Each hour they let
consciousness go out and their color

of purple with it. No concepts,
no possessions, no anger of loss.
Nothing to release but their

quickness of life. They let it go
slowly into brown, into the whisper
of the sere, the soft, eroded yellow.

NOCTURNE

The light was driven across the grass, out
of the trees, out of even the field of the park.
It went through into a place I could not see
and the vibrant white roses just after.

The breeze which spelled the words passing
between the acanthus leaves fell back,
drew the last reflected shadows deep
into the bowl of its own transparent eye.

Each of these changes became but a single
turning in a sandless glass of memory
as the first thin edge of moon took a cloak
of stars down upon itself as easily as Diana

had taken it for a bow so many lives ago.
I was lifted into a drifting night mist
of speechless shape, a rhythmic flowing
across and melting of place, as if need

and all idea had been drained from my pen
out onto the lines of that page, remained
there, absorbing, assuming, about to sing
in unrepeatable, wheel-shaped cadences.

UNDER LIMBS, UNDER CLOUDS

Sickness, winter, I had been long indoors.
Just around the corner behind stone gates,
in the place of park below the reservoir,

ancient apple trees were offering white blooms
to the seamless, unreserved sky which itself
was the blue and white of high, streaming

clouds. They both were free in a light
they seemed to be meeting for the first time.

There in that linking of unbounded energy
I felt radiant with the hungers of youth,
the forgotten, because not for so long heard,

phrases of hands, of arms, of the uplifted
heads of lost loves, opening their eyes

to reveal a network of multiform memory
rich and foliate like blooms, like clouds
coming down from very high up, gathering

over themselves and seeming to offer
a picture of the ageless face of longing.

THE GOING BACK

I was small then and my mother appearing
in the darkness with the light flowing in
and curving around her, seemed large,
the perfume from inside her dress

surrounding all my senses, the white
that was the upper line of her breasts
showing above the edging of dark lace
and drawing a force I could not name

out from inside me. My mother was large,
my father large, the entrance to my school
as broad as the space behind my dreams.
The playground, itself, rolled away

an incalculable distance. One tree stood
in the furthest corner. I went toward it
with open eyes. Many leaves had fallen,
lay at the bottom of the flagstone

tree well. They were each the yellow
and bright orange of summer, receiving
the brittle, autumn hand of winter,
and one leaf larger than the rest,

with brown ridges wrinkling at its edge,
almost covered the grey stone fallen
out from the wall, sunk in the earth.
Now it is autumn and autumn again,

thirty-seven years since I knelt,
braced my hands against the ground,
leaned all the way over to look in.
The day is ending, a single teacher

holding a cloth notebook, passes down
the hill, is lost in layers of dusk.
In a few steps I cross the schoolyard.
Standing, bending at the waist, I lean

over once again, receive into sight
the dense, clumped roots which weave
like arteries in and out of the soil
and under the walled blocks of granite.

The yellow leaves are not there,
only the long teeth strokes of a rake
which has been pulled like chalk
across a broad blackboard, then washed

with rain. The one stone remains,
I see it is small and worn, almost round.

WAKING BY THE LAKE

Kisses and other first instinctive touches,
fall in arcing profusion upon her limbs
lying in the lake, as I rinse her with caresses.
A transparent glowing connects us both,
though the shore is now only a longing
pointed toward where we thought we began.

And in the wash of these waters we do not
need protection, like the child Moses floating
secretly, safely, on his bed of braided rushes.

The guns grow louder as the birds come in.
We lie there watching. Many are killed
but many come behind, landing two, three,
four, on each broom-flag stem of reed.

Evening and the hunger of hunters fills
itself in with them, becomes luxurious,
like the knotted spaces left in vine-thick air.
Arm in arm we turn over, sink deeper.
I cannot stop breathing her name,
her skin, the flesh of even her feet,

as this ceaseless, almost profligate
arrival of wings turns to the piercing
cry of bodies beating against the walls

of their own form, settling themselves down
like a leaded cloak over the one eye
of our two lives. We hold without sound
to the shifting, dark shape of that place.

SEEING THE TURTLES RELEASED NEAR DEVON

When I saw them set loose in the surf near Devon,
swimming free under the billowing, heaped-up,
grey and white clouds of a Constable-like
English sky, I thought of you pulling those waters
past yourself with the strokes of your arms,
parting it with your head, letting your hair

ruffle and stream out wide. I knew light
would flood into your heart, as it did into mine,
at the thought of those large turtles loosed
from the tanks of the aquarium, the glass sides
of which seemed to open a world of foreign eyes,
where, though they pressed their weight forward

they could not enter. Then to see them depart
in the darkness of rubber-lined wooden boxes,
see them carried a long distance, lifted out
in an instant at the edge of the surf, walk
with feet in actual eddies of sand, straight
into that endless flow, the many grasses bending

with the green weeds, wave tumbling over wave,
rain falling straight onto rain, as they took
the stippled waters into their own arms, felt
their shells surrounded with it, were borne up,
barely needing to eat or breathe, were drawn
north along shores which once were beaches,

valleys spreading undersea, full mountain slopes
which now hold no trees, stand in waters so dark
day can express itself only within the muted
shapes of dusk and night, were drawn south from there
into shallow aquamarine lights where knobby
coral reefs and blue, orange, yellow fish seem

to retain glistening memories of sun, even
in the last hour before dawn. Gautama Buddha
once said, it is as difficult for a human
to be born as a human again, as for a single
bull floating in the world's ocean to put
his head into a single yoke also floating.

It this is so, within the wideness of time,
let us travel for centuries in the sea, after
the seemingly inevitable end of this speechifier,
man-womankind, who talks of freedom, clear waters,
pushes measureless leavings of waste out into
the broad-roaring and the blue pacific oceans.

There coming 'round some wave-washed island bluff
or out from under a long escarpment shelf,
we may meet the far-ranging turtles, gaze
each toward the other in a sea without sides,
exchange looks in the clarity of freedom, of pure
traveler's sight, continue our wordless journeys.

MORNING TRANSIT

I turn the corner, turn down the concrete drive
into the garage and into the front seat.
Start the engine, set the gear. No thought.
Two minutes, perhaps, without thought.
Cross the street, stop at the light. White

blossoms. Perfect blooms crowding on the limbs
in such a full pushing out and completion
of tree energy there is no room for leaves,
only occasional dark edges of bark showing
beneath. The day begins to rain large drops.

One bloom loosens, drifts to the ground.
The air seems pulled apart. In a single moment
a small flaring of white has fallen down
from the breath of the living into the frame
of solitude, as a thought is spoken then passes

through a distance it never imagined, cannot
carry forward. The truth of unrepeatable act,
not simply beauty or loss, sounds within me.
The light changes. I get out, pick up the bloom,
lay it on the carpeting between the seats.

Its perfume of pollen fills the car. Now
I have one thought. In this age of killing
and the fear of being killed, of a deep
hungering after the comfort of objects and then
the full fracturing of matter by machines,

I will celebrate the subtle life of changes,
spread the vinyl seats and metal, make room
for the nameless place of becoming, leave
this bloom and every description of it, free
to depart, never frame them in this way again.

PENNSYLVANIA STATION

Horns and the tearing, mad syllables of arguing.
Car tires and steam-driven hammering and each
of your words, fiery and announcing, as if
this were a completely wired city and it were
exploding around me. We enter Penn station.

My eyes are drawn into a bond with the suffering
of those sitting in rags or in very old
blankets, on papers or on the bare cement floor
where puddles of dribbled out body water
reflect a dim light which seems to lift

from their last threads of energy. It is cold.
We walk by as if we cannot understand, cannot
explain, find ourselves wanting to believe
that suffering is inevitable, and even, perhaps,
an inherent part of this passage of the breath

into and out of our bodies. These bodies
which we think of as living shells covering
something we call the soul, and which, itself
finds its form beyond the flesh, beyond first
memory, outside of the interstices of change,

as if one of you whom I have loved
had turned your eyes back to me as you passed
behind a wall, out of a door, signaling that you
would not be far away but were nevertheless
separate, somewhere else, and finding the code

of your life woven into other lines, while
at the same time you drew the veil which radiates
clear, thin shafts of hope close around yourself,
maintained the belief that one day this human
struggle would clear off, find its balance,

and each of us would be lifted up from the room
of our solitude, out of the fractured road
of search, return as if as one to our lost,
harmonic selves. There, at that moment
we, each, would finally be linked to the other

as if we were the strongest and most
compassionate of friends, and this world then
might no longer press its face in upon us
as though it were a dark and corroded, barely
open mirror, on which in falling, incorporeal

lines of water we feel compelled to write
the hundred varied injustices of daily time.

ARCTIC SNOWFIELDS SEEN FROM THE AIR, LONDON FROM THE STREET, DECEMBER 1983

On the Occasion of the Harrod's Bombing

Between a field of grey and white cloud
lying on white crevassed snow, and a sky
peeling upward and releasing itself hour
by hour into blue and cobalt blue and black,
between these two seamless faces changing
continuously and gazing into each other,
the sun rose, crossed between, shortly set,
in many hours rose again, a pale flame, both
close in and far off like the face of a dream.

And what else, and what else was there
at the top of the earth in that shifting
whiteness where one felt weightless, free,
and able, almost, to step into the lights
of the heavens. No trees were there, nor
none of Poe's ravens crying, NEVERMORE.

Each flake lay unique against the one next
and that polar ice cap whose length
no man had ever walked, whose breadth
no man had ever fully seen, that immense
trackless expanse lay silent, measureless,
the last earthly field without anger.

And amongst us in the cities where buildings
rise like trees and like trees are slowly
stained, fade and fall, there is a hunger
which does not end: the fierce whispering
of lost hope breaking close within, exploding.

Now in the London of traffic signal lights,
where Burne-Jones and the Pre-Raphaelite brothers
sang the harmonies of the pure soul, the hollow
boom of metal tearing metal goes on broadening.
Christmas, and thick, winter clothes of shoppers
flutter down like wind-frayed prayer flags
onto the roofs of cars and covered dust bins.

Children lose their mothers' hands, and flesh
is torn loose from flesh, as cordons of police
come forward to screen off the curious, alone
at last as they had always wished, with the sight
of a suffering deeper yet than their own.

The shredded bone is covered with white sheets
and detectives save the twisted ribbons and scorched
presents for inspection. And what else, and what
else is there where matted hair and fringes
of ears lie alone and bleed through smoke?

Spirit has always spoken to spirit across
the disappearing centuries, as if with the flame-
like intensity of Northern lights, but now
the fractured face of death stands between.
Catholic, Protestant, Irish Marxist, urban
guerrilla, you each must draw back from each
and from the ponds and streams, the turtle and fish
are in the waters and the fibrous reeds cannot
feed upon the acid weight of bomb-charged rain.

Snow will be falling when at last the last
turtle dies. He will not be able to drink
his own inward, crystalline song, and only
those few of us who can breathe and hold
our warmth within the inverted cold of Northern
lights, will not be alone, ended as we are,
and lying here motionless on this street.

THE SECURING OF THE SEEDS

You're just like all of them, she says,
wanting to be recognized, have your name
edged in lights. She leans back into
the cushions lying on the sofa, looks

intently at me. No, I say, we are all
like them, waiting to be seen, be heard,
have our short length of identity
brought into form so that we can believe

one, or better, many others cared for us.
But what of the earth? It could be giving
all of itself to the arrival of the sun
into this long winter of North America

as if it were human like us and were held
in the clear hand of a complete love.
Trees could be flowering in each street
where asphalt covers the seed bed even

as it drifts down from its branches
of broad scattering, builds its deep but
expungeable base of pods and flying pollen.
Covered alive while living, without light,

without oxygen, while we continue driving
painted steel machines across the range
of its face, eating ice cream and demanding
that others acknowledge our individuality.

Is she still listening? I see I believe
this moment of history sits as if waiting
on the edge of ruinous change, and I have
almost naively chosen myself, mere

words that I am and carrying the print
of an older voice, to reveal the knowledge
that together we can change, together
we can draw back, leave this earth to every

shape of its remembered self. Our hands now
can free themselves of weapons, our bodies
give up products manufactured by force,
paper made from motor-cut trees whose grain

had taken centuries to complete, food
formed from the flesh of cows, chickens,
kept in corrals and cages, medicines
made from tests performed upon animals

whose organs and limbs were cut open
while they were living, small monkeys,
each one as gentle and as clever
as the fingers of a child's hand, large

monkeys, chimpanzees, mice and white rats,
dogs, cats, even wolves, all of them
borne away in canvas bags, in the backs
of trucks, to the common city dump.

All of it arrogant, careless. No
plant or animal truly opposes itself
to us. The only wars are our wars,
the only acts held in the airless

room of administered death, our acts,
as we go on killing and covering over,
cutting ourselves off from the oxygen
of the forests. Now she is sleeping,

and I see I can no longer believe
this man-constructed city will be able
to give up the taking of life in the
name of science. I no longer believe

we can turn toward simplicity, choose
the unadorned clarity of labor, the many
rhythms in which hand coordinates
with eye and the body frees its trapped

energy, looses its weight of toxins,
leaves the seated forms of comfort
scattered like drying shells behind it.
Speak birds, burst outward seeds,

go forward and whisper in her ear
you restless, up-thrusting mountains,
we need full, unconditional waking
in each of the rolling, blue-green seas.

THIS PRESENT LIFE

The sun is setting out at the edge
of my known world, beyond the tall hedges,
orange, dark orange and a soft, open red.
And high up, flaring as light, as a kind
of loose irregular halo, fading airy pink
washing against a pure stream of white.

Each cast of light lights each glass
on the table, crosses through the opposite
window, strikes from the goldenrod, as if
it were a note from a large bell, its own
inherent yellow. Walking out the door
I see small, completely solid, black beetles
moving through its scalloped leaves, along

round stems, over curving horn-shaped
blooms, eating. Smooth-paced and regular
in motion, they push forward with jaws
hidden far underneath, shred the veined
leaves, work the fibers in rolling motions
down the short length of their bodies, eat.
Even before the light changes I go in.

Water is boiling. I put in fresh corn,
I sit down to chicken soup and crackers,
each one snaps in my hand as I break it.
Strange, unknown words rise within me,
are these the varied shapes from which I am
to bring forward the inextricable mystery
of the named and the unnamed of this world?

LATE SUMMER

When occasional drops of rain fall only sharply,
as if forced from narrow openings in the sky,
and stones hold those drops as liquid shelter
against the sun, and leaves not yet touched

by frost, leaves eaten then by tent worms,
fall in slow, descending strokes like the long
pull of heron wings, then I find myself calling
to them in what feels like their own sound.

Then, gradually, I am calling upon the sun
to descend so I can freely choose the dark
and not begin to seek it. Slowly it is clear
that this is the furthest curve of turning,

mists become my constant search, shadows
the remembered shapes of all my thoughts
set against the heat. Now it is late summer
in the unrecovered longing of my life,

I also will depart. The moon if I can choose
will be in crescent, a pure sounded note,
a door drawn in the form of a curve
and holding every direction of memory.

THE PLACE OF COUNTRY

Like blood the congregating weight of body fluids
flows out from me in streaming chains, yellow-
green acids filling the white, enameled bowl.
From within this sealed envelope of myself
I see I am simply a membrane to food lines
which enter and depart. I sit down to write,
words slip away like unreadable memories.

I lie down to sleep, dreams end in questions:
Did young Werther wander in the fields of Saxony
with anguish trailing after him? Did Paganini
play Polish Nocturnes with tears cresting
at his eyelids? Was that sentimentality?
In every office room we whisper against
each other. And still in late-night bars

I can feel the hidden hungering for weapons.
And with the sadness which sleeps within
we sometimes touch, walk on. Did we not injure
one another as surely with our personality
shifts as with the padded truncheons of prisons?
Fall against us death so that we may hold
to our last thoughts of peace. For myself

I seek to depart from anger, see that I am
in country, hear the barely remembered swaying
of trees. See that there are many fewer of us
and we live together scattered on the hillsides
singly and in such unity as the blades of grass.
See that I live in fields set among large
stones, make drawings of the simplest things,

a clay cup holding milk, a small cat
drinking from it, a flint oblong in shape
and weighted pot-like toward its bottom
with its mix of ores. Each of these glows
from within and holds its form where the sun
crosses through, frames them without effort
in the motionless unfolding of its presence.

ENTERING THE DREAM

Early morning in a sky filled with smoke
and the fog of dawn. I am delivered from air
into the walls and hallways of the landing
terminal. The sun that blinds, lights at once,
stains the drifting clouds red and passes
into my eyes as I walk in fatigue, feel
the first whisperings of molecular fall. John,

Service Maintenance Corp., stands dead already
where the liquid detergent flows in one line
down from his plastic can, spreads across
the scarred linoleum. Dead as his stomach
swells over his brown belt and he lets cigar
ash flake continuously onto his chest. Dead
as his wife called to him to pick up the milk

and his youngest son screamed as his brother
poured dust over his black curls and the door
closed slowly on what he had not ever felt
was home but his one dream fallen through
into broken chairs, washed-out, cracking plaster.
Each of us, looking back at the other, sees
we have sunk into the gravity of time where

older hopes fail and find their place within
sequences of decay. We long for nothing, stop
seeking, feel the long slopes of the bowels
imperceptibly invaded, give in and weaken
like a moment which wishes always to be present,
then is gone in a ticking of clocks, crawling
cancers and the several other sediments of loss.

He turns back, spreads the cleanser out in angles
from the center, as the car door opens to take me
down from hotel towers and maintenance hangars.
Far off from here I can see a single stream
and sloping field gone wild into brush and vines
and tangled hedges. I step in mind through its
waking breath, feel grass giving life to hundreds

of birds, mice, swarming bees, and red there,
alone among the separate shades of green,
small blossoms shaped like inverted bells
and growing almost numberless in the intricacy
of their cluster. They seed themselves, take
root, drink the chemical rain and synthesize
the dark, exhausted air. Enduring, indomitable,

speaking their lives in red, I bend and pick
one as talisman, walk on through the grass
toward the stream lying flecked with paper.
It is there with the flower set in my jacket
I sit down to see the morning, see the padded
ends of my fingers turning greenly to tendrils,
my feet adding bark and blending as a trunk

into the ground. Time cannot be measured.
I am gone far off with Ovid and the dream
of the ancients. I join the growing world
as a tree of living flesh, leave this seeking
after the artifacts of satisfaction, these
cars inanimate and manufactured constructs
imprisoning the speechless stems of the senses.